WHERE THE SOUL BLEEDS

Lavanya Jalan

ISBN
Paperback 979-8-89632-843-8
Hardcase 979-8-89699-341-4

CONTENTS

ANGELS LIKE YOU

You hold my hand like it's something to save,
A tether to keep me from the waves.
Your love, a lighthouse, steady and bright,
But I am the storm that drowns the night.

Your eyes see the best in this chaos I am,
A heart made of cracks and a soul of quicksand.
You build me up with your gentle grace,
Yet I'm the wreckage you can't erase.

I wish I could be the calm you deserve,
Not the sharp turns, the unsteady curves.
But breaking is easy—it's all I've known,
And you're too good to reap what I've sown.

Your laughter feels holy, your kindness divine,
While I'm tangled in shadows that poison the vine.
You deserve a love that's pure, that's free,
But angels like you shouldn't fall for me.

I'll ruin it all; it's just what I do,
Turn gold into rust, taint skies with the blue.
Yet even as I tear us apart piece by piece,
I'll love you forever, and hope you find peace.

YOU'RE NOT LESS

In the quiet of the night, when all is still,
A voice awakens, one that's hard to kill.
It's the voice that knows your deepest fears,
And feeds on every pain, every tear.

It starts as a whisper, soft but clear,
Reminding you of every flaw, every fear.
It points out the scars, the cracks, the mess,
Convincing you that you're somehow less.

You stand before the mirror, searching for peace,
But all you see is a puzzle with a missing piece.
The reflection stares back, eyes full of blame,
As if to say, "You'll never be the same."

You wear your smile like armour, thin and weak,
But underneath, you're tired, fragile and frankly meek.
The thoughts run wild, relentless and cruel,
Making you feel like a broken fool.

But when that voice whispers you're not enough,
Remember that surviving is tough.
And though the scars will always be a part,
They don't define the whole of your heart.

SELF-WORTH

There isn't a day where the war pauses,
not one where I can carry love for myself
through all 24 hours.
It slips, falters, fades like a fragile thread,
and in its place, the familiar weight of disdain settles in.

These thoughts—they knock,
and I don't even resist.
I let them enter,
let them speak their cruel truths,
let them unfurl and weave themselves
into the fabric of who I am.

"You're unworthy," they whisper,
and I don't argue.
I bask in the ache,
let it settle deep,
because somehow, it feels deserved.

If a person spoke to me
the way I speak to myself,
I'd never keep them near.
I'd slam the door,
walk away.
But I can't walk away from me.

It's not that I judge the world—
I love its mess, its imperfections.

I try to see the beauty in others,
to hold them with kindness.
But when it comes to me,
the lens shifts,
the kindness turns sharp.

I hate the way I walk,
the way I speak,
the way my thoughts race and trip over themselves.
Even the things I create—
my hobbies, my words—
feel like pale imitations of worth.

How cruel it is,
to live in a body you loathe,
to inhabit a mind you can't escape,
to carry a heart that beats
while it whispers that it's not enough.

I wonder sometimes,
what it would feel like to forgive this flesh,
to accept this mind as it is.
But the thought feels distant,
like a star I can't reach.

So I sit with the hatred,
let it rise, let it fall,
a tide I don't know how to stop.
And somewhere in the quiet of its ebb,
I wonder if there's a version of me
that I could ever learn to love.

UNREQUITED LOVE

I love you like the sky loves the stars,
boundless, aching, from afar.
Yet you remain, shimmer on the horizon,
a shadow cast across my vision.

We are parallel lines drawn by fate's careless hand,
always near, yet never to land.
Your laughter is a melody I try to hold,
but the tune fractures; it grows cold.

You are the sun, untamed and bright,
I, the moon, drifting in borrowed light.
Caught in your orbit, I falter, I wane,
sinking in quicksand, tied to pain.

Each glance from you is a thread too thin,
a lifeline fraying where hope wears thin.
You don't see; your eyes skim by,
like the wind brushing leaves that sigh.

I speak in silences, my words concealed,
an artist whose canvas stays unrevealed.
Each heartbeat whispers a hollow plea,
a prayer to a god who turns from me.

Still, I love, with a love that bends,
like roots that grow where the earth descends.
For even as I sink and cannot move,
this unspoken love, I'll always prove.

Though we are paths that never converge,
you remain the dream I cannot purge.
An eternal ache, both curse and bliss,
a story told in a fleeting kiss.

MOTHERS

I used to think
it was duty that kept her close,
a weight she carried
because she had to.
I was the burden she never asked for,
something to hold, to bear,
because that's what mothers do.
But now, I know better.

I know how her words can cut,
sharp as glass,
and I try to hold the panic down
each time she says them,
try to keep the pain at bay.
But I can't.
Her voice lingers,
etching itself into the hollow spaces of my chest,
and I carry it like a stone.

"You're a mistake," she says,
and the words slam into me,
again and again,
like waves that never stop.
I try to tell myself she doesn't mean it,
that it's the anger talking,
the exhaustion, the years of sacrifice.
But the way her eyes look through me,

like I'm nothing,
makes it hard to believe anything else.

I hear her love in whispers,
soft as a lie.
"I love you," she says,
but I can feel the weight beneath it,
the anchor of her resentment.
It pulls me under,
drowning me in the truth
she doesn't have to speak.

She despises me.
From the bottom of her heart,
she despises me.
And no matter how much I don't want to,
I believe her.
I always will.

Every moment becomes a reckoning,
her voice the judge,
the executioner,
and I am the crime.
Even when I try to hold myself together,
to knit my broken parts into something whole,
her words unravel me.
Her disapproval seeps in,
coiling around my ribs
until I can't breathe.

She's more than just the blood
that runs in my veins.
She's the shadow over my heart,
the second heartbeat
that pounds with panic and fear.

Without her,
I might still be here—
breathing, walking,
a hollow thing among the living.
But with her,
I am less than this body.
I am less than survival.
And even when I don't want to,
even when it tears me apart,
I believe her.

NEVER QUITE ENOUGH

I try to be the best I can,
To give my all in my life's span
But somehow, I'm never right,
I'm always left alone at night.

I wear a smile and try to hide my tears,
I know I'm strong cause I face my fears,
But this harsh truth I've always known,
I'll never be enough, not on my own.

I just don't quite understand,
Why everything I do or say,
Just pushes them all away.

I try to give my heart, my soul,
but at the end, I'm always told,
That I'm too much or not enough,
This journey oh it's always tough.

I try to love with all my heart can give,
I dream, I hope, I dare to live,
But here I stand, alone again
Climbing yet another hill,
Wishing that one day I'll meet
Someone who finds enough in me.

CALM

She hated life but feared to leave,
A quiet ache she couldn't relieve.
Each day a struggle just to breathe,
Yet still, she stayed, afraid to grieve.

She loved the sound of love's soft song,
But felt that love had done her wrong.
She'd listen close, her heart held tight,
Yet never knew that warmth, that light.

She laughed with friends, her mask in place,
But tears sat hidden, no embrace.
A smile she gave, though it was thin,
Hoping to cry, but kept it in.

Her heart, though full, remained alone,
A distant place she'd never known.
She carried weight too much to bear,
Wishing someone, someday, would care.

In every tear she never shed,
In all the words she left unsaid,
She wandered lost, not wanting more,
Just seeking calm amidst the war.

SINKING

There are days when the thoughts come so fast
they pile up in the corners of my brain,
like a room filled with smoke,
thick, suffocating, impossible to see through.
It's like I'm trying to speak through glass,
the words rising, pressing against my throat,
but nothing escapes.

I can feel it,
the pressure building,
a dam about to break.
It's all too much—
the endless worries,
the what-ifs, the unknowns,
all of it clings to me like a shadow I can't shake.

And then, it's like water.
I'm sinking, slow at first,
but now it's pulling me down,
deeper and deeper,
my lungs filling with the weight of everything I can't say.
I don't know what waits at the bottom—
a salvation I've been too scared to reach for,
or a silence so heavy it will break me.

I want to move, to breathe,
to make sense of this storm,
but the fear freezes me in place.
It's as if my body is caught in quicksand,
the more I try to fight it,
the deeper I sink.

And so, I let the water take me.
I sink, wondering
if I ever speak the words out loud,
will they set me free?
Or will I drown in the silence
that's been waiting all along?

THE ABSENCE OF LIGHT

I held your hand through the storms in your mind,
Each wave of chaos, each moment unkind.
You lashed out in anger, a tempest unplanned,
Yet I forgave, again and again, as I'd always stand.

"It's not your fault," I whispered to the night,
Convincing myself it's just absence of light.
Your need was a hunger I couldn't fulfil,
For it wasn't my love, but the pills and the thrill.

Your eyes, once soft, now hollow and vast,
Haunted by shadows of the choices you cast.
I fought for you fiercely, but the war took its toll,
And now I'm just ashes, a shattered soul.

Where's the line between love and despair?
When caring feels like a noose you wear?
I tell myself it's not darkness I see,
But this absence of light is swallowing me.

Yet, here I remain, tethered and torn,
Caught between hope and a love over-worn.
I can't leave, though I'm breaking inside,
Still searching for the spark where shadows collide.

But maybe the light was never in you,
A truth I can't bear, but know is true.
So I sit in this dusk, between wrong and right,
Telling myself it's just absence of light.

THE ESCAPE

When my nose is buried in my book,
I slip into new worlds,
where skies shimmer
and characters come alive.
Here, everything feels lighter,
each word a step forward,
each chapter a door wide open.

But the moment I close the cover,
reality slams shut behind me
the silence grows heavy,
my own heartbeat echoing,
a relentless drumbeat of anxiety,
the familiar demons circling back,
dancing on the edge of my thoughts.

I feel the weight of the walls closing in,
the edges of my mind fraying,
and I am trapped,
not in chains, but in echoes,
caught in the labyrinth of my own making.

I crave the escape of those pages,
where struggles are conquered,
while here, I wrestle,
each breath a battle,
each moment a question
with no clear answer.

Yet, still I seek the next story,
the next portal to freedom,
because in those fleeting hours,
I am not trapped,
I am alive
a traveller of dreams,
opening my wings
one word at a time.

Now I understand why George Martin said,
a reader lives a thousand lives
cause each tale is a refuge,
a world where I can be
more than just plain old me.

TO BE A POET

To be a poet, you need
A heart that's heavy and a soul that bleeds
Like Van Gogh's ear and Hemingway's gun,
They carved their beauty from their pain
until they had nothing left to give.
I wonder why their wounds
Are what taught them to write
As if the beauty of their art
Must be derived
From their tragical pain
That their hearts couldn't suffice.
Yes, I have enough pain
Enough wounds for a lifetime's sake
Dead friends and fears that always linger
But what if I don't want the weight of despair
These things that haunt me late at night
What if they aren't really there?
What if beauty and art could go hand in hand?
And you didn't need ugly insides
Or broken souls to make them rise.
Maybe it's time to change
This old wife's tale
That to fill pages with ink
This emptiness you must feel
One that leaves you so broken
That you can't fathom coming back.

HOW WAS IT?

They greeted me, bright-eyed, eager,
their voices a chorus of warmth.
"How was it? How was life?" they asked,
as if I'd just returned from a journey
too grand to put into words.

"It was fine," I said,
watching their faces shift from joy to confusion.
Fine.
The word tasted like ash in my mouth.
I should have said more, I knew.
But what?

"No, tell us," they urged,
their voices insistent, almost desperate.
I felt their light pressing on me,
their hope unravelling the knots of my silence.
So I said it, all of it.

"You want to know? It really wasn't that great.
I finished school, found a job,
but could barely afford to live.
I spent so much time worrying—
about money, about people, about myself.
I felt betrayal from everyone I trusted.
Never found true friends, never saw much of the world.
I guess I didn't even live."

The room, or whatever heaven is,
grew cold in an instant.
Their faces turned pale,
their radiance dimmed by a shadow of something
I couldn't name—grief? Shock? Guilt?

"What did we do wrong?" they whispered,
their voices trembling like brittle glass.
"What could we have given you
that you'd see the beauty we poured into every day?
The joy in open skies,
the symphony of birds in the morning?
What more could we have done
to show you the miracle of being alive,
to make you notice the light,
not just the shadows?"

I stood there, their words
a weight I didn't expect to carry.
And maybe I was angry—
at them, at myself, at everything.
But mostly, I felt hollow.

"I don't know," I said.
"Maybe I was too busy trying to survive
to see the sunsets you painted for me.
Maybe I was too scared, too hurt, too tired
to stop and breathe in the beauty
you scattered all around.

Or maybe," I said,
my voice cracking under the weight,
"you gave me life,
but you never told me how to live."

And in that silence,
as their grief rippled through eternity,
I wondered if heaven was the place
where you finally learn
how to love the life you left behind.

LOVE'S NOT COMING

I sit by the window most days,
not really looking at anything, just waiting.
It feels like I'm nobody's to find—
like I've been left here by mistake,
waiting for a person who took a wrong turn
or forgot I existed.

Sometimes I wonder if I'm invisible,
like the world passes by and no one looks up,
no one sees me sitting here,
waiting.

I put a stethoscope on my heart last night,
just to check if it's still beating,
because some days it feels quiet inside,
like everything stopped
but I didn't notice.

I keep thinking I'll hear footsteps
or feel something shift in the air,
like love is supposed to make an entrance—
grand, unmissable.

But all I hear is silence,
and the air is still.

I watch people fall into love
the way they fall into step with each other,
easy, like they knew the rhythm all along.
And I wonder if I missed the lesson
or if I'm out of sync,
waiting for music that never plays.

I tell myself it's fine,
that maybe love isn't meant to be found,
maybe it's not for everyone.

But sometimes, late at night,
when the world is too quiet,
I listen to my own heartbeat
and wonder how long it will keep waiting
for someone who isn't coming.

I ASKED GOD

I asked God to give me wisdom,
He said, "No, it doesn't work that way,
You'll find wisdom in your struggles,
In the mistakes you make each day."

I asked God to make me stronger,
He said, "No, strength isn't just given with ease,
For strength is earned in the weight you bear,
In the moments that bring you to your knees."

I asked God to bring me peace,
He said, "No, peace isn't handed out,
You'll discover it in quiet times,
When you learn to ease your doubt."

I asked God to fill my life with love,
He said, "No, love isn't just received,
You'll create it in your kindness,
In the hearts that you've relieved."

I asked God to make me happy,
He said, "No, joy is something earned,
You'll find it in the simple things,
In the lessons you've discerned."

I asked God for another chance,
He said, "No, I gave you life to use,
So make the most of every day,
It's up to you to choose."

So I stopped asking for more,
And God smiled and said to me,
"You've got everything you need inside,
Now go, and let yourself be free."

THE VOICES DESPITE THE SILENCE

I sit in rooms full of voices,
words pounding at the edge of my lips,
but I swallow them down,
bitter like bile,
sharp like secrets never shared.
I've grown used to the quiet,
not the peaceful kind,
but the kind that sticks to my ribs
like a sickness I can't shake off.

Each time I open my mouth,
someone else's words rush in,
filling the air where mine should be.
I let them.
I've learned to listen,
not because I want to,
but because it's easier than the taste of rejection.
I know this silence too well,
better than my own voice,
because every time I speak,
I'm afraid the world will turn away,
afraid they'll leave, like before.

Their laughter becomes my silence,
their opinions, my empty nods,
and my thoughts grow heavier,
like stones in my throat,

weighing me down, sinking me deeper.
So I let their opinions settle on my shoulders,
like borrowed coats I never wanted to wear.
Their choices shape me,
carve out pieces of me,
until I barely recognize the person lost in the crowd.

I used to fight it,
once had fire in my chest,
but now my heart drops just a little more
each time I let someone speak over me,
a piece of me breaking off quietly,
like chipping away at the edges of a cliff.
It's not that I don't have thoughts—
I have too many,
but each time they rise,
I push them down,
because I know how it feels to be the outcast,
and it's a cold I don't want to face again.

It's who I've become,
a people pleaser, they call it,
but it's more like drowning,
swallowed by the waves of everyone else,
until my voice is a whisper,
too faint for even me to hear.
So I've taken this vow of silence,
not out of peace, but of fear,
because it's easier to be quiet

than to pick another fight
I've grown too tired to win.

And every time I hold it in,
I taste it—
that bitterness,
like acid on my tongue,
reminding me of all the things
I never said,
and all the moments I let slip away.
I've learned that when I speak,
the words stumble,
and the apologies come faster than the anger ever did.
Sorry, I say,
for having a voice,
sorry for daring to think.

So now I hold it all inside,
a storm waiting behind locked doors,
but at least in the quiet,
I don't have to fight to be heard.
At least in the silence,
no one walks away.
I'm losing myself,
piece by piece,
but that seems like a small price to pay
for staying in the warmth of belonging,
even if it's not really mine.

Because I'm not ready
to stand on the outside again,
to feel the cold against my skin,
and so the silence—
as suffocating as it is—
still feels safer
than being alone.

DEVIL INSIDE

A flicker of flame in the dark of my chest,
A storm on the rise where I dare not rest.
A whisper, a hiss, a voice in the night,
The devil within me, unseen but in sight.

I walk on the edge, where shadows collide,
Between who I am and what I hide.
Chains of temptation that cling to my soul,
A fragile facade—trying to hold control.

There's fire in my anger, there's calm in my rage,
I'm both the bird in the cage and the cage.
I fight with my demons, yet hold them so tight,
The devil in me, drawn close in the night.

But maybe the dark is where truth starts to grow,
Where pieces we bury begin to show.
And so I dance with the devil inside,
An echo, a warning, a place to confide.

Perhaps I'm the spark and the blaze and the fear,
The devil within, both distant and near.
A haunting, a healing, a path I pursue—
I am what I fear, and I'm what I'll undo.

UNMASKED

I've learned to live with hunger's claws,
a gnawing silence, sharp with flaws.
Days without food, then one bite too much—
every swallow a bruise, every calorie a crutch.

Mirror whispers, cruel and clear,
"Shrink a little more, disappear."
But tell me this—
I don't draw lines on my heart to change its size,
or paint my pulse to brighten my life.
So why do I sculpt my bones to meet
a shape that leaves me incomplete?

I carve and shadow, cast myself small,
just skin and shell, and still not enough at all.
I smooth on powders, erase each line—
but every shadow hides a lie.

These hands—they've trembled, clenched, they've fought
to hold what I am, against what I'm not.
If starving brought peace, I'd have found it by now,
but all it leaves is hollow vows.

See me, raw, unpainted, fierce—
no mask, no frame, no need to pierce
this fragile flesh, this worn disguise.
I am whole beneath the lies.

POISON

Once, we were children,
full of wonder,
our minds soft as clay.
The world was vast, uncharted.
We touched it with curious hands,
tasted it with open mouths.
We ran through the grass barefoot,
unknowing of the shadows that lay ahead.

Our parents,
with their warnings,
their caution like an old chant—
"Be careful with the screens,"
they said, "the machines will steal your spirit."
We laughed then,
for what did they know?
They feared what they didn't understand.
We,
we were the future.

But time has a way of showing
what words cannot.
Now, we sit,
not children anymore but hollowed adults,
fingers fused to glass,
eyes glazed over with code.
The world shrunk,

not vast anymore but pixels,
binary,
feeds,
notifications.

They told us
we'd be limitless.
That the whole world would sit in our pockets,
and it did,
but it sits so heavy now,
its weight pulling us down,
anchoring us
to this virtual ground.

Do you feel it?

Do you feel it now?
The way it creeps inside,
taking root in our thoughts,
replacing our memories
with algorithms,
our dreams
with simulations.
We thought we were building it,
but it has been building us,
restructuring our brain,
layer by layer,
turning flesh into metal,
thought into data.

We carry it with us,
this poison,
we know now,
but still we drink.
Willingly,
eyes wide open,
hands reaching for the next fix,
because freedom, freedom is too terrifying.
We are not what we were,
but what else can we be?
The warnings still echo,
faint,
but we can't hear them anymore.

Our brains have learned another song,
a song we cannot forget.

TURTLE SHELL

Every time I'm hurt,
or angry,
or lost in the haze of my own bad mood,
I become something I don't recognize—
a creature that wields love like a weapon.

I take the secrets they trusted me with,
those fragile pieces of themselves,
and I turn them into arrows.
I aim where it will hurt the most.
And when the damage is done,
when the air is thick with their pain and my regret,
they leave.
They always leave.

So I taught myself to leave first.
Not physically, but emotionally.
When the storm rises in my chest,
I pull away,
close the doors of my heart,
retreat into the hollow safety of silence.

I've become a turtle,
curling into my shell,
letting the world pass by
because it's easier to be alone
than to risk hurting them again.

But silence is its own kind of violence,
its own kind of betrayal.
I push them away with my quiet,
with the walls I build higher every time,
until they don't know how to reach me anymore.

I tell myself this is better.
This is safe.
But sometimes, in the stillness of my shell,
I wonder what it would feel like
to let someone stay,
to trust myself not to destroy them.

Maybe I'll learn, someday,
how to hold my anger in my hands
without letting it burn those I love.
Maybe I'll find a way
to be something other than a storm.

CELLS ANEW

I found out today that
Within three months, our skin renews,
A fresh start where our touch once bloomed.
Cells that felt your warm embrace,
Now are replaced, they leave no trace.
Does that mean you've slipped away?
No touch, no warmth, no sweet relay.

I wonder if you think of me now
Of the moments we shared now tinged with pain
No longer do I feel your hand,
But memories of us in the back of my mind
They still stand.

When I think of what we had,
which I once believed was love oh so true,
Now stained with bittersweet memories
Of your schemes that pierced me through.

Now you've left, with well
No tangible touch, no physical trace,
Cause my cells are anew
All I have are the echoes of our love now misplaced

Our history fades, yet lingers on,
In my memories you're never gone.
Though my skin may now forget,
My heart holds on with deep regret.

EMPATHY TO APATHY

People say, "Try to put yourself in others' shoes."
Well, I've been trying my whole life,
Trying to feel empathy for others' pain.
I think I've been void of this emotion too long,
Now I've stopped feeling empathy for my own hurt, my own pain.
The empathy that's supposed to be there has been replaced
By apathy's cruel embrace.

I try to break other people,
Try to see if that will help me feel for them,
But my feelings refuse to show their faces,
Leaving me lost in these empty spaces.

I know this makes me heartless,
And I almost think that I am.
That I've been broken far beyond repair,
My heart has endured too much despair.

I think it's built a wall of stone around it,
Refusing to feel, not one bit
For it has endured far too many icy hands
That felt joy in crushing its tenderness, my gentleness.
And now they're gone, replaced by this cool indifference
And icy numbness, a chilling persistence.

TV

I don't want to talk right now,
The news is louder than my voice somehow.
Every word feels rehearsed,
Like I'm trapped in someone else's verse.

The world's on fire, it's on every screen,
Protests rage where the grass was green.
But I change the channel; I look away,
Who am I to save the day?

Maybe it's selfish to turn it down,
To mute the chaos, ignore the sound.
But I can't bear to feel this small,
A single thread in a crumbling wall.

They're airing trials like it's a game,
And everyone's choosing sides to blame.
I scroll and scroll, a passive gaze,
My life reduced to endless plays.

I put on a sitcom to drown it out,
But even the laughter is wrapped in doubt.
Behind every punchline, a weight so real,
A joke can't change the way we feel.

I used to dream of making things right,
But now I just sit here, bathed in light.
Maybe tomorrow I'll break away—
Turn off the TV and face the fray.

IF I HAD FIVE LIVES

In the first, I'd stay with my parents,
not just as their child but as their equal.
I'd listen—really listen—
to their laughter, their silences, their stories.
I'd try to understand who they are
outside of the roles they play.
I'd do good for others, as they taught me,
but mostly, I'd try to be good to them.

The second life would not be mine.
It would be theirs—
their dreams, their fears, their expectations.
A steady job, a husband chosen
not by love but by duty,
children in a house that feels too small
because my soul would not fit.
A white picket fence around a life I didn't build,
but one I'd maintain.

In the third, I would break everything.
I'd smash through walls I built in fear,
chasing the rush, the fall, the unknown.
Skydiving, diving deeper,
letting fire kiss my skin
or the ocean hold me too long.
I'd push until my body gave way,
just to feel what it's like to let go.

The fourth life would be soft.
No regrets, no rules, just love.
I'd stay with friends who feel like sunlight,
fall in love without wondering
if it's forever or fleeting.
Every moment would be a feast—
every laugh, a symphony.
I'd see beauty in cracks,
joy in the smallest things.

The fifth would be solitude.
A camper in Iceland, parked under endless skies.
Books would become my lovers,
words my only company.
I'd write poems in the quiet,
the kind that feel like prayers.
With dogs at my feet and the world far away,
I'd watch the seasons pass
until I, too, became part of the stillness.

Five lives to live,
each one a different shade of me.
But here I am with just one—
and somehow, it feels like enough
to try for them all.

IT WASN'T MEDUSA'S FAULT

It wasn't Medusa's fault,
Yet her beauty became her bane.
Poseidon's hunger left her defiled,
And Athena, blind with disdain,
Turned her hair to serpents' coils,
Her gaze a weapon of pain.
The god walked free, untouched, unmoved,
While Medusa bore the stain.

Sita walked through fire's embrace,
To prove her heart was pure,
A trial by flames for Ravana's crime,
A pain she must endure.
Rama's love was bound by doubt,
Her worth became unsure—
She was made to leave her kingdom's care

For a life she did not deserve.

Eve, they say, unleashed the curse,
Though she was led astray,
By whispers from a serpent's mouth
In Eden's golden day.
Adam's hands were clean, they claim,
His blame was swept away—
And so the burden of the fall
On Eve was forced to stay.

Hester wore the scarlet mark,
For sin she did not bear alone.
Dimmesdale, her lover, hid his shame,
Behind the priesthood's stone.
Yet she endured the public scorn,
Her child, her love, her throne—
While men of cloth and rigid laws
Threw hearts against the stone.

Pandora opened a gilded box,
A gift the gods designed,
To unleash plagues upon the world,
And chaos on mankind.
Yet it was Zeus who planned the trap,
His vengeance intertwined
Still, they cursed her curious hands,
And left his wrath behind.

History and lore, unkind to women,
Write them villains, mark their fall.
Erase the names of those who wronged them,
Or let them stand proud, tall.
Blame the victim, spare the power,
This cycle haunts us all.
But hear these voices, fierce and true:
It wasn't Medusa's fault.

YOU AND I

You are the sun and I am the moon
Your light shines bright while I fade too soon
We walk different paths
You're the day and I'm the night
Yet my heart longs for you, your warmth, your light
You are the summer so full of cheer
I am the winter so cold and clear
You laugh and dance in the sun's embrace
Yet I watch in silence feeling out of place.

You are the fire you burn so bright
I am the water the cool and quiet
You burn with a spark which I hold down
Yet I still dream of your touch.

You are the ocean so vast and free
I am the shore that's longing for you endlessly
You come and go with the tide's flow
Yet I still seem to be waiting for you.

You play melodies so sweet and pure
Yet I am the silence still unsure.
But in your song, I hope I find my place,
A quiet harmony in your never-ending grace.

IN BETWEEN

Caught in the tide, a half-grown soul,
Not quite a child, not fully whole.

As a child, I never dreamed of escape,
But now I'm caged, longing to reshape.

A shadow floats between grown-up rooms,
Where laughter's stale, and duty looms,
And childlike corners left behind,
Where games now seem too far, confined.

Yet here I am, half-formed and torn,
Yearning to be what I have yet to mourn—
To shed this skin, to race ahead,
Yet tangled up in fear and dread.

Caught in flames of nostalgia's burn,
For the days when life took a simpler turn,
Where joy was boundless, and tears would fade,
Not wrapped in doubt, mistakes half-made.

How do I hold what I can't understand?
My own mind's a storm I can't withstand.
Barely knowing what I feel inside,
Yet expected to keep others satisfied.

Speak too much, and I'm out of place;
Stay silent, I vanish without a trace.

Every word a dance on shattered glass,
While I'm trying to find the strength to last.

And freedom—oh, how it calls to me,
To be unbound, yet whole and free.
But freedom's a dream on the edge of night,
An aching wish just out of sight.

It's tiring here, this breathless place,
A middle ground, a nowhere space,
Where dreams feel close, yet out of reach,
And finding words feels like defeat.

A voice too big, yet small inside,
A gentle push, a place to hide.
Someday, maybe, I'll find the way,
To be enough, but not today.

BELIEFS I NEVER CHOSE

When I was young, they spoke of Santa,
The jolly man with a sleigh of dreams.
I believed, though I never saw him,
For their words were the truth, it seemed.

The tooth fairy, soft as whispers,
Slipped coins beneath my pillow's care.
No proof, no sight, yet I trusted,
Their stories shaped the world out there.

But now, as a teen, their words still linger,
Not of magic, but of anger's flame.
"You're lazy," "You'll fail," "You'll never matter,"
Echoes etched beneath my name.

No sleigh bells ring, no fairy dances,
Yet these phrases root within my core.
Unproven truths, but I still believe them,
Wounds reopened, bleeding more.

But what if those words, like Santa's stories,
Are just shadows cast in running light?
What if the mirror doesn't know me,
And I am more than their angry night?

For maybe I am endless like the sky,
Not the clouds that momentarily pass.
I am more than the sharp-edged whispers,
More than reflections in fractured glass.

So, I'll rewrite the tales they've told me,
A kinder script where I belong.
Belief, it seems, is like double-edged magic,
And I'll wield it now to make me strong.

BLOOD RUNS THICKER THAN WATER

Blood runs thick, thicker than water,
a bond unbroken, a love that won't falter.
Its call is fierce, its ties are tight,
a bond that holds both day and night.

It speaks of names, of kin, of pride,
of love and duty, side by side.
Yet waters surge with wild force,
they wander free, they change their course.

I'm pulled between these ancient ties,
the roots below, the open skies.
For blood, it binds, a heavy chain,
while rivers dance through sun and rain.

Blood holds the past, the tales, the pain,
it knows my flaws, my loss, my gain.
But water calls me far from here,
to paths unknown, to skies so clear.

Blood may anchor, water roams—
one keeps me still, the other homes.
In blood, my history flows thick;
in water, freedom's gentle trick.

Both hold me close, yet let me go,
in roots below and streams that grow.
So here I stand, both bound and free,
where blood and water flow through me.

YOU KILLED ME

In English, we say *you killed me*,
but in poetry, we speak in flames.

I burned like a candle,
steady, soft, and alive—
and you came as the wind,
a gentle breath at first,
then an untamed howl,
leaving darkness where light had been.

In English, we say *you broke my heart*,
but in poetry, we speak in edges.

You took love's blade to my spirit,
sharp and certain,
and carved me into silence,
each word unspoken
a scar on the tongue
I no longer dare to use.

In English, we say *you left me*,
but in poetry, we speak in shadows.

You were the sun against my skin,
golden, fierce, too much,
and now I walk in twilight,
a creature unseen—

learning how to live
without the light that burned me.

In English, we say *goodbye*,
but in poetry, we speak in echoes.

Your name is the sound
that lingers in empty rooms,
a fading note from a song
I never wanted to end.

In English, we speak plainly,
but in poetry, we make art
from what destroys us.

And so I write you—
a wind, a blade, a shadow, a song—
because poetry is the only way
to love what is gone.

THE WEIGHT WE CARRY

I once believed my pain was mine alone,
a shadow cast only by my sky,
an ache carved into the marrow of my bones,
sharp as winter winds, relentless as tides.

But the world is a mosaic of hidden grief,
and now I see—
each person is a book
with chapters they won't let us read

And each person carries a suitcase
filled with secrets too heavy to unpack.

The girl who smiles wide in her photos,
her hair cropped close—
"Trying a new look," she says.
But I know, somewhere,
there's a battle her scalp remembers,
and chemo whispers the truth
behind the hashtags.

The boy laughing loud at the party,
is he drowning out his doubts?

The mother who stands like a pillar of stone,
her cracks filled with silence,
holds the weight of worlds she cannot drop.

Pain seeps into us all,
like rain finding the smallest crack in stone.
Wounds, no matter their size,
bruise and bleed and sting the same,
binding us all in an unseen kinship of ache.

This world is made of sorrow and bliss,
a trembling balance we all must keep.
So I remind myself:
no matter how heavy my heart feels,
how unworthy,
how alone—
there are others carrying weights
I'll never see,
fighting battles I'll never know.

And perhaps that's the point,
to understand that we are woven
of the same frangible threads,
maybe we are constellations of broken stars,
lighting the same vast sky,
burning quietly with shared stories,
each flicker of pain is proof that we belong.

www.ingramcontent.com/pod-product-compliance
Lightning Source LLC
LaVergne TN
LVHW091236150826
845673LV00003B/1165

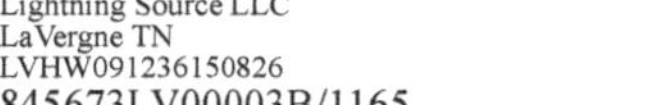